Nursing Homes for Italian Americans in New York City

FACTORS FOR UTILIZATION

Rosaria Musco

Library of Congress Control Number: 2019937629

Calandra Institute Transactions
Volume 4

ISBN: 978-1-9393230-9-5

John D. Calandra Italian American Institute
Queens College, CUNY
25 West 43rd Street, Floor 17
New York, NY 10036

CONTENTS

ACKNOWLEDGEMENTS

I am extremely grateful to Dr. Anthony Julian Tamburri, Dean of the John D. Calandra Italian American Institute, for his unfailing support of my professional development and for recognizing the importance of publishing this work.

My heartfelt thanks also go to the staff of the Calandra Institute who have been my cheerleaders. Special thanks to: Lisa Cicchetti, Siân Gibby, Itala Pelizzoli, and Carmine Pizzirusso; your knowledge and skills have been indispensable in seeing this work to fruition. Thanks also to Dr. Donna M. Chirico, Professor of Psychology and Dean of Arts and Sciences at York College/CUNY, for her expert advice.

In addition, I would like to gratefully acknowledge my Capstone adviser, Dr. Elizabeth Eisenberg, for her invaluable insight and her keen sense of guidance, as well as the CUNY School of Professional Studies and the CUNY School of Labor and Urban Studies/The Murphy Institute.

Lastly, I dedicate this work to the people who inspired it: my late grandmother Rosaria Mazzella and my family.

PREFACE

This research examines factors that may influence the use of nursing homes by Italian Americans in New York City. Some of these factors include whether elders are afflicted with mental or physical disabilities, and whether family members of elders need to work, making them unable to take care of their elders in the home. This research looks at participants of Italian American descent, aged sixty-five years or older, and who live in New York City.

What is evident from the published literature is that first-generation Italian Americans are not likely to place their elders in nursing homes or assisted living facilities. There is a strong sense of duty to take care of one's elders at home. There seems to be a shift with second- and third-generation Italian Americans. Although the family bond is still very strong, there is more of an acceptance of placing one's elders in a nursing home or assisted living facility, or of obtaining paid help. Findings from this research may be useful to the Italian American community as well as to family members deciding on future placement of their elders in nursing homes or in assisted living facilities.

CHAPTER 1

INTRODUCTION

> Studies of aging among racial and ethnic groups such as blacks, Chicanos, and Japanese-Americans have increased dramatically in the last 10 years, but the experience of so-called "white" ethnics remains relatively unexplored by gerontologists. The immigration of Europeans into the United States has increased during the last three decades. This is especially true in the case of Italians and Greeks . . . An exploration of the available literature on white ethnics and aging reveals a paucity in material. (Fandetti & Gelfand, 1976, 544)

Italian Americans have been part of the fabric of this country from the beginning; they have made tremendous contributions to the growth of the nation. The literature reviewed in this research shows that there are no nursing homes or assisted living facilities in New York City that cater predominantly to the Italian American elderly population. In part this has to do with the beliefs that Italian Americans have towards their elders. The only facility close to the kind I describe is a Senior Citizens Housing center in Brooklyn, built by the Order Sons of Italy in America (OSIA). According to their website, OSIA is "the oldest national organization for people of Italian heritage in the United States." Cav. Joseph Sciame, one of the past presidents of the organization, stated that OSIA came up with the first $10,000 to build the facility, and the U.S. Department of Housing and Urban Development (HUD) funded the rest. This was approximately thirty years ago. The families who live there do not receive assisted living, only rent assistance. Sciame also said that because HUD was involved, the facility is open to all ethnicities. Although the housing center is owned by OSIA, they do not administer it; a management company takes care of it. Sciame believes this was a great investment for OSIA; after twenty-five years they were able to refinance it, and monies that they took out were used for scholarships, educational programs, and cultural programs. Sciame also said, "Ironically, when asked and invited to do another upstate site, at the time the Executive Board in its 'wisdom' rejected it, feeling that the investment of $10,000 would not be worth it. Today, we would have millions! Oh well, the short-sightedness of some!"

Traditionally, in Italian American families the elderly are taken care of at home by their children, specifically by their grown daughters. This leads to the title of this research: *Nursing Homes for Italian Americans in New York City: Factors for Utilization*. Some of these factors might include mental disabilities or physical disabilities that make it difficult for elders to remain independent. Another important factor in determining how elders are cared for include whether family members need to work full-time. Those who can afford it will get at-home care, which is costly. Such a difficult decision regarding elder care might perhaps be made easier if facilities like a nursing home or an assisted living facility existed that catered specifically to Italian Americans.

Findings from this research discovered that Italian Americans prefer to remain in their own homes. They prefer to have paid help come in if needed. If they did have to enter a nursing home, then one that catered to their ethnic and cultural background would be welcomed to make the transition easier. Respondents preferred the idea of living in an assisted living facility over a nursing home. The respondents also made it very clear that they value family bonds. In addition, my research showed that the majority of respondents do not have any plans in case they should become incapacitated. This is, after all, a subject that many people do not wish to ponder or discuss, and Italian Americans are no different in this regard.

Of the 2,551,995 Italian Americans living in New York State, there are 117,405 who are sixty-five years and older living in New York City (Public Use Microdata Sample American Community Survey, 2014). No other research has explored the reasons behind the lack of an Italian American nursing home in New York City. The purpose of this research is to establish whether or not there is a need for such a facility, but also to shed light on the lack of scholarly literature regarding elder care for Italian Americans. In addition, conducting this research will begin the conversation for future research, not only in relation to the Italian American community in New York City but potentially to all ethnic minority elders in the United States.

Based on very limited research done thirty-six years ago, data showed that first-generation Italian Americans were more likely to live at home with their children than second-, third-, and fourth-generation elders: they were more likely to be placed in nursing homes or have at home care. However, some examples of data about other ethnic groups who hold the same basic beliefs as Italian Americans do about their elders show that these other groups have been successful in creating an environment where their elders can be taken care of in the manner suited to their background.

This research focuses on Italian Americans living in New York City and evaluates the results of a survey of those who are sixty-five years and older to find out whether they would be interested in entering a specifically Italian American facility while they are still physically and mentally able. The focus of this research is to discover if there is in fact a need for Italian American nursing homes in the New York City area.

STATEMENT OF THE PROBLEM

There are plenty of nursing homes and assisted living facilities within New York City, but none that specifically cater to the Italian American population. In addition, as we shall see there is a very large gap (thirty-six years) of scholarly literature conducted on elder care for Italian Americans. Aside from a chapter in a book, or an occasional newspaper article, this subject has not been explored. Such a shortage of research has made it difficult to ascertain the needs of elderly Italian Americans.

Italian Americans in general have found it difficult to place their elderly in nursing homes. First-generation Italian Americans are used to the idea of taking care of their elderly at home. In part, the choice to provide care for elderly in the home might have to do with the costs involved for placing a loved one in a nursing care facility. According to the New York State Department of Health, the average cost for a nursing home stay in New York City is $395.00 per day, or $144,395 for a year. A price tag this high can make the cost prohibitive in many cases. Additionally, Italian Americans for the most part revere the elderly, and there is a stigma attached to nursing homes for Italian Americans.

Contacts with middle-aged Italian Americans indicate often their bond with older relatives is unwritten, motivated by duty or repayment, and sometimes by love. The possibility of a parent becoming totally dependent can create considerable anxiety for Italian American adult children. Community sanctions as well as filial values make nursing home placement a most undesirable option in many families. Relatives frequently worry about what others will say if they decide to place a parent in a nursing home, as nursing homes are often seen as existing for those without a family. (Kolb & Hofstein, 2007, 121)

Families today have a great struggle. Those who can afford it will get at-home care for their ailing parent, and those who do not work outside of the home will take care of their ailing parent. This in turn puts a huge strain on that person's family, for it is never easy to take care of someone who is ill, whether physically or mentally. In addition, depending on the illness, in-home care might not be sufficient, the elderly person might need more dedicated medical care making placement in a nursing home a must. All of these questions become more complex when an elder does not already live near their family members.

Second- and third-generation Italian Americans seem to accept more willingly the option to place elder family members in nursing homes. This is sometimes an outcome that emerges if children have moved away from their parent(s) and do not live in close enough proximity for regular visits or constant care. A key question for this research is whether a medical or nursing facility that caters to a specific ethnic background might make an elderly person more comfortable and less ambivalent about seeking elder care in a facility outside one's family home. Is there a need for an Italian American nursing home in New York City?

PURPOSE OF THE STUDY

The purpose of this research is to shed a light on the gap that currently exists in research on Italian American eldercare and to begin to fill that gap by looking at how Italian Americans in New York City think about eldercare, what their concerns are about the future. Undoubtedly, a better understanding of the cultural and practical concerns for this community will encourage the establishment of options for eldercare that would meet the needs and preferences unique to the Italian American community.

CHAPTER 2

LITERATURE REVIEW

The number of Americans sixty-five years and older is quickly increasing. According to the American Association of Retired Persons, "The U.S. sixty-five-plus population is expected to more than double to ninety-two million by 2060." In addition, the number of the elderly ethnic minorities in all developing countries is also rising. The needs of these minority groups are different than the needs of the general population of that age. In the United States, one sub-group of the elderly population is Italian Americans. In light of the fact that limited studies exist pertaining to this group, this research explores which factors influence the utilization of nursing homes by Italian Americans in New York City. Presently, the ethnic and cultural needs and the religious beliefs that characterize this population are not identified or addressed by health professionals and long-term care facilities.

Studies by Fandetti and Gelfand (1976) and Gelfand and Fandetti (1980), argue that first-generation Italian Americans tend to take care of their elders at home, unless the elders have a loss of mobility or are bedridden. However, studies have not been conducted to analyze whether first-generation Italian Americans would care for an elder at home if the elder had Alzheimer's disease.

A more recent study conducted in a single medical center in Rome, Italy, by Vellone, Sansoni, and Cohen (2002) describes the experiences of informal caregivers who take care of family members who are affected by Alzheimer's. It evaluates six factors:

changes in relationships, changes in lifestyle, difficulties in caring, hopes and fears for the future, family duty, and respectful treatment. The authors state:

> Caregiving for people with AD [Alzheimer's disease] has been widely studied in other countries, especially in the United States, but little knowledge of this topic exists in Italy. Studying this topic can help families better cope with their roles. Because cultural differences exist between countries, the international literature may have only limited application to AD caregiving in Italy. (324)

The study indicates that family members have little knowledge about the disease and they experience a lack of support from the Italian National Health system. All caretakers expressed feelings of inadequacy and concern that their care of and behavior toward their loved one may contribute to their family members' decline. Additionally, the families interviewed expressed a strong belief in God's power to improve their family situation. Under these circumstances, the family of a person with Alzheimer's disease takes care of the aging family member at home. It is important to note that in Italy there are no known facilities equipped to care for patients with Alzheimer's disease. Perhaps this is due to the family bond of taking care of your own regardless of what ailment one might have. Vellone, Sansoni and Cohen (2002) report that these caretakers felt a sense of familial duty, along with a commitment for respectful treatment of the elder person. These two factors are among the beliefs that Italian immigrants took with them the U.S.

Although the limited research available in the United States illustrates that Italian American family bonds are still very strong, how elders are being cared for has changed. The literature suggests a lack of diversity in healthcare staff as well as a paucity of research pertaining to elderly ethnic minorities and racial disparities in the United States and in all developing countries. In addition, the literature indicates that half of the population age sixty-five years and older suffer physical ailments including a fractured hip, loss of mobility, and dementia.

ITALIAN AMERICANS, POLISH AMERICANS, AND JAPANESE AMERICANS

Much of the literature on Italian Americans, Polish Americans, and Japanese Americans shows that all three groups revere their elders and that all possess a strong filial bond. The study by Fandetti and Gelfand (1976) surveyed family members between the ages of twenty-one and fifty. Fifty-one women and forty-nine men were interviewed. Within the sample, 15 percent of the participants were Italian and 18 percent were Polish. Both groups belonged to the same socio-economic background. The average age for respondents of each gender was forty and thirty-nine respectively. Researchers found a high ratio of first-generation immigrants in the survey. There were nineteen foreign born Italians and eight foreign born Poles. There were eleven respondents with minimal command of the English language. The respondents were asked to evaluate several situations. For example, individuals were asked about their attitudes toward nonfamily long-term care. Of the respondents 45 percent said it was acceptable for elderly needing intensive physical care to be in an institutionalized facility. Within this sample, 82 percent indicated that their relatives would not be comfortable living in a care facility where the staff was of a different ethnic background than their own. This was mainly due to the majority of the elderly relatives not speaking English, making communication difficult. The respondents assumed that the elderly relatives would not be able to adjust to different cultures and custom. Interestingly, this shows that through time the language was valid in 1976, but based on the research conducted for this study language today was not an issue. Nonetheless it shows that even in 1976 there was interest in an ethnically based medical facility.

Respondents were asked to rank the order of preference they had regarding which method of long-term care they preferred for their elderly relative. The choices included the Catholic Church, local ethnic organizations, the State of Maryland, the Welfare Department, and private organizations. Fifty-seven percent chose the Catholic Church as their first choice and 29 percent chose as a first preference the local ethnic organizations. The remaining 24 percent favored the other three outside institutions. The respondents regarded the Catholic Church organizations as a trustworthy place that would provide great care.

Respondents were asked if nurses outside of the ethnic community could be trusted in caring for their elderly, and 72 percent said that they saw no reason why nurses outside of the community would not take care of their elderly in the same way as a nurse within the ethnic community. Respondents felt that a nurse is a nurse regardless of her ethnic background. However, both Italian and Polish families had a sense of family obligation and therefore would prefer to have their elderly be taken care of by their own. Only when their loved one required ongoing medical treatment and they felt unable to take care of their elderly in the proper manner were family members willing to seek long-term care outside of the home. Notable is the fact that second- and third-generation respondents showed more of a preference to seek outside care for their elderly than first-generation respondents. According to this study, a possible explanation for this disparity is the fact that second- and third-generation respondents had a higher education and income level. Also, this difference could partly result from the assimilation of these generations into mainstream America and hence the acceptance of assisted-care facilities as an option.

Respondents were asked to evaluate the difference between facilities and caretakers: The perception differs between Italian and Polish Americans. Whereas Italian Americans did not trust the outside healthcare professionals, Polish Americans did not have an issue with this. According to the authors this is also another possible area of research, that variations exists even among what would appear to be similar ethnic communities. The authors say that according to the data collected in this study, in the future potential utilizations of institutional facilities will become part of these communities as a choice for their elderly. The researchers further suggest that since the majority of respondents were in favor of having the Catholic Church being involved, that option should be explored. Even in this there is a difference between the generations; first generation immigrants are willing to utilize a facility run by the government.

The authors point out the importance of examining ethnic and religious subgroup characteristics to make sure social policies and programs can also be adapted according to their specific needs. This is a very important point, given the fact that present findings of this research still show a lack of scholarly literature in all major developing countries, the United States being one of them.

A subsequent study done by Gelfand and Fandetti (1980) analyzed a sample of one hundred and thirteen middle-aged Italian American men living in the suburban area of "new town" Columbia, MD. Both studies looked at the traditional structures of family, church, and ethnic organizations. The authors noted that the study of the suburban Italians is not representative of the Italians nationally, and that demographics and socioeconomics and the attitude of the Columbia samples represent middle-class individuals in the suburbs.

Researchers reported that the Italian men living in Columbia were overwhelmingly professionals and highly educated; 83 percent had either college or graduate degrees. More than 50 percent had a family income of more than $30,000, and 75 percent of the sample showed marriage with other ethnic groups. This was in opposition to the Baltimore study, where the respondents' education was at the high-school level at best, and the household income was $10,400. It was also noted that the parents of the Columbia residents did not live nearby; in fact 60 percent lived more than two hundred miles away, whereas in the Baltimore study parents and family lived within walking distance. Respondents were asked questions about generation and living arrangements: Both the Columbia and Baltimore respondents showed an increased preference for independent living for their elderly. While second and third generations preferred independent living for the bedridden elderly, Columbia residents responded that institutional care was preferred; in fact, 60 percent of the third generation of Columbia residents preferred institutional care.

Instead, for the third-generation Baltimore respondents, only 31 percent preferred institutional care for their bedridden elderly.

Respondents were given five choices of long-term care for their elderly: State of Maryland-run, Welfare Department-run, Catholic Church-sponsored, local ethnic organizations, and private proprietary groups. The Catholic Church in this case was still the most preferred; actually the preference for the Columbia residents was even higher. Respondents in both Baltimore and Columbia rejected in large part the idea of a facility being operated by the welfare department, and only 12 percent of the Columbia respondents preferred ethnic run organizations having an organization like the Order Sons of Italy viewed as not appropriate to take care of the elderly. However, Baltimore respondents were 29 percent more likely to be in favor of such an arrangement. The Columbia residents also seemed to incline toward the use of proprietary organizations as a long-term care option for their elderly. Notably, third-generation Italian Americans who reside in Columbia are less inclined to choose church-run organizations; instead, nursing homes are on the rise for this group.

When respondents were interviewed on whether or not they felt that their elderly relatives could be comfortable in nursing homes operated by staff of different ethnic backgrounds, 56 percent agreed that they would. These Columbia residents were also not raised in an ethnic neighborhood, and one of their parents was not Italian American. In contrast only 18 percent of the Baltimore group felt the same way. This is a notable difference from the 1976 study. Also, it accords with my current research where the majority of participants' comments indicated that they were mostly concerned with the care they would receive from a facility and not so much if the staff had a different ethnic background than theirs.

STABILITY AND CHANGE IN ATTITUDES: INTERGENERATIONAL HOUSEHOLD UNITS

It is notable that both the Baltimore and Columbia residents still rely on basic family support to assist the elderly. Also notable is the fact that among the Columbia residents who were more educated and had a higher income, their preference was for the elderly to live independently. Third-generation Italians of both Baltimore and Columbia prefer their elderly living independently as do the elderly themselves. This current research supports this statement as well.

Some studies have suggested that the third and fourth generations of Italian Americans in the next decade or two will increase their migration rates toward the suburbs, to fulfill the American dream of their forefathers of owning a home.

The authors note that although these changes are happening, it still does not diminish the family responsibility toward the elderly and that family assistance is still a very strong preference among respondents. What does change is how white ethnics are caring for their elderly and that some decisions about care are becoming less traditional.

Based on the research by McCormick, et al. (1996), first-generation Japanese Americans also felt that their elders needed to be taken care at home given the strong support system that is in place there. However, both Issei (first-generation Japanese Americans) and Nisei (second-generation Japanese Americans) based on responses from a questionnaire were more than willing to have their elders enter a nursing homes if dementia were to set in (although this group also would consult with their religious leaders). As researchers point out, this willingness is also due to the fact that Keiro Nursing Home, which caters to the cultural needs as well as the physical ailments of the elderly Japanese Americans, was built in the Seattle area. Another point of interest is that the second-generation Japanese Americans were willing to enter or place their elders in a non-ethnic nursing home.

Although the family bonds for all these groups are still strong, the literature also indicates that as time goes on attitudes toward caregiving for one's elders are changing. This change is due to a number of factors, principally assimilation into American mainstream. Sons and daughters alike are moving away from the neighborhood they grew up in and seeking higher education, obtaining more demanding jobs, and taking ownership of homes—therefore, moving away from the traditional care that could once be provided by families to their elders.

NURSING HOMES, HOSPICE CARE, AND RACIAL DISPARITIES IN ETHNIC MINORITIES

The literature reviewed in this section discusses how racial disparities have effected care of ethnic minorities in reference to end of life care, do not resuscitate (DNR) orders, and do not hospitalize (DNH) orders. The literature findings indicate how important it is for healthcare services to become culturally and gender sensitive to the needs of this growing elderly population. They also point to the language barrier that exists for some ethnic minorities, as shown in the 1976 study of Fandetti and Gelfand on Italian Americans, where respondents of the study felt that since the facilities did not speak Italian their elderly would not be comfortable or able to communicate with the staff. This is an important issue, since miscommunication already exists compounded by lack of language knowledge can lead to misdiagnosis and misinformation.

The study conducted by Duffy, et al. (2006) looked at end-of-life preferences of Arab Muslims, Arab Christians, Hispanics, blacks, and whites in Michigan. A total of seventy-three participants were registered at total of ten focus groups were conducted. In 2004 a conference sponsored by the National Institutes of Health concluded that more studies needed to be done to include more minorities in research by using various methods of collection. This study showed that Arab women felt uncomfortable out in the open in a public hospital since their customs require that they always be covered. Findings indicated that most blacks did not personally experience discrimination but talked about past discrimination of someone they knew or had heard of, and white women complained of abandonment by healthcare professionals once one is dying, while white men instead experienced age discrimination. As this study showed, end-of-life preferences vary greatly depending on racial/ethnic background and religion, from all measures being taken to prolong life to withdrawal of life support and assisted suicide. In addition, all groups when discussing end-of-life care expressed a desire for all business taken care of and communication with doctors to be done with respect to their spiritual beliefs.

Research has suggested that the racial disparities that persist in nursing homes about end-of-life care documents are due to race cultures. In the study by Degenholtz, Arnold, Meisel, and Lave (2002) the data covered 3,747, residents in nine hundred and fifty two facilities and an academic medical center in nursing homes across the United States. The study found that the average nursing home resident is sixty-five and over; half were female; almost all residents had been living in nursing homes for three years; nearly half of these residents were afflicted with Alzheimer's disease or other dementia. The study also found that 58 percent of nursing home residents had some type of advance care plan. Some of the comparisons with the different races revealed that white non-Caucasians and African Americans were less likely to have a DNR/living will. Hispanics were less likely than Caucasians to have DNR orders. The researcher conducted this study by having a quantitative approach with the use of sample weights used for generalization of 1.56 million residents in 16,840 nursing homes, and it used only publicly available data. Secondary analysis of public data was conducted for this paper; the sampling was from the 1996 Medical Expenditure Panel Survey Nursing Home Component.

Additional literature comparing the use of hospice care services among African Americans, Latinos, and European Americans in South Jersey covering the years 1995 to 2001 showed that hospice care services were underutilized by ethnic minority groups compared to their numbers in the general population (Colon & Lyke, 2003). The authors also discuss some of the differences and similarities of these groups. Out of these groups neither the African Americans nor the Latinos were likely to have family members who would help in their care, whereas the European Americans had a family member or spouse that would help in their care. And the Latinos were most likely to have a family support system. Payment methods also differed; European

Americans were less likely to use Medicaid than either African Americans or Latinos. European Americans were more likely than Latinos to use Medicare as a form of payment. The research also showed that all three groups were most likely to die at home and therefore no significant difference was noticed. The researcher believed that the underutilization of hospice services by these minority groups is most likely due to the lack of diverse staff as also mentioned in Duffy et al. (2006) where researchers recommended that the staff of long-term facilities be culturally trained about the growing diverse elderly population. This study shows the lack of literature on the subject of Italian Americans. It is impossible to determine if Italian Americans were part of this study, given the broadness of the term "European Americans."

SCHOLARLY LITERATURE'S NEGLECT OF ETHNIC ELDERLY MINORITIES

A number of studies have looked at the scholarly literature that is available on the ethnic elderly minorities both internationally and in two of the leading geriatric journals.

As reported by a study originating in the United Kingdom by Mold (2005), 25,166 ethnic elderly are in care homes in England and Wales. First, the findings of the international literature report that the United States had sixteen studies, three from Taiwan, three from China, two from Canada, and one from Australia, and, second, the findings of the United Kingdom literature that only three journal articles came from the United Kingdom. A total of twenty-eight journals are included in this review paper. Two of the UK studies were dissertation abstracts originally from the United States. Gray literature and policy documents originated from the United Kingdom. The inter-national literature describes how important the transition from home to care homes is for individuals. Maintaining family ties is crucial. This is all critical in maintaining a sense of self-identity and worth, which in turn helps residents adjust to their new life and can make their care treatment effective. This is also true for Italian Americans who, as shown through this research, still value family bonds. It also points out the question of and the potential need for an Italian American nursing home, since the transition from independent living to a facility is not easy for anyone, and thus if there were a facility that catered to one's ethnic back-ground it might make the transition easier to accept.

The international literature also highlights the difficulty that family members face as part of family obligation versus the inability to take care of a loved one for a number of reasons: cross generational differences, cultural changes, etc. The literature found in London points to disparities of social and healthcare needs in minority ethnic elders. A greater participation on the part of the Ethnic Minority Forum and the Refugee Network has been summoned. It was also found that there is a need for healthcare workers to participate in training workshops on cultural diversity programs as mentioned in the studies of Colon and Lyke (2003) as well as Duffy et al. (2006). In addition, although all these methods of culturally caring for an ethnic minority play a role, the most important one is the language barrier. The author of the study (Mold, 2005) believes that if translation services are available to ethnic minority elders then they can not only communicate their needs and likes and dislikes but their care can be better suited to them.

The next study that focused on the scholarly literature about elderly ethnic minorities examined two publications, *International Psychogeriatrics* and *International Journal of Geriatric Psychiatry* covering the years 2002 to 2006 (Shah, Doe, & Deverill, 2008). Simple descriptive statistics were used to locate and identify the number of publications dealing with ethnic minority elder groups. Only original research was considered, and other items such as articles, editorials, review, abstracts, commentaries, and letters were excluded. Two of the authors took on the task of examining the two publications. The results showed that: 7.6 percent (66) of the publications looked at ethnic minority elders; 5.1 percent (44) of publications were only about ethnic minority elder groups; and 2.5 percent (22) of publications included minority ethnic elder groups in their sample. The authors gave various reasons for this "paucity" in the literature including that researchers might not want to work in this area due to language barrier. The bias and prejudice of researchers toward this specific population might also be a factor. The authors say that some reviewers of geriatric psychiatry are not given favorable assessment, most likely due to the fact that the methodology used to conduct research in minority ethnic elders is at an early stage of being developed and the inclusion in any study might make data collection more complex. The authors point out that there is emerging literature pertaining to "ethno-psychopharmacology" of different ethnic groups in their respective country of origin. The researchers found high numbers of "ethno-psycho-pharmacology" studies in ethnic minority groups in any given country.

CONCLUSION

As the literature shows, the needs of elderly ethnic minorities are not being met by long-term-care facilities, nor are services adequate for this population. More research is needed to develop geriatric care methods that will adequately address current needs of these populations. There is scarce research available regarding the subgroup population of Italian Americans, with the exception of the two studies mentioned here. The studies, by Fandetti and Gelfand (1976), and Gelfand and Fandetti (1980), provide the most current data on Italian American elders. This thirty-six year gap in research strongly suggests that more current studies are needed.

The remaining literature analyzed for this review has no direct reference to Italian American elders. In the Fandetti and Gelfand (1976) study, Italian Americans are among those labeled "White Ethnics." Other studies identify groups as "European Americans" or "Non-Caucasians." The ethnic identities of these groups are not specified. Therefore, it is not known for certain whether Italian Americans are included in ethnic minority studies. This lack of ethnic detail has made the available research difficult to assess, further indicating the need for more up-to-date data.

This research shows that Italian Americans, Polish Americans, and Japanese Americans share a reverence and respect for their elders, and the first-generation families in these populations prefer to care for their elders at home. Among second- and third-generation Italian Americans and Japanese Americans there is more acceptance of placing their elderly in nursing homes. A Japanese-American community in Seattle has further responded to the cultural and physical needs of their elders by building the Keiro Nursing Home.

Both the Fandetti et al. studies (1976 and 1980) and this current research have demonstrated that second- and third-generation Italian Americans are content with having their elderly taken care of by nonethnic caretakers or facilities and do not feel the need for such a facility to cater to the specific needs of the elderly Italian American population. As the authors of the 1976 and 1980 studies have suggested, Italian Americans have attained full assimilation into American mainstream society. The assimilation process that has been sought out by first-generation Italian Americans for their children may have influenced and shifted attitudes and respons-ibilities of caring for one's elderly family members.

This apparent lack of research on Italian Americans (indepen-dent variable race/gender) and their attitudes toward care of the aged and the different types of care (dependent variables) prompted this author to begin the process of researching the stated title in this study.

CHAPTER 3

METHODOLOGY

RESEARCH PROCESS

The research process is as follows: A questionnaire was created to target those who are of Italian American heritage and sixty-five years old and over with open-ended questions (such as: *If there was a nursing home that catered to the Italian Americans would you be willing to live in it?; If no, explain; If yes, explain*). In addition, the questionnaire asked individuals if they wanted to be contacted for interviews to aid this research.

The questionnaire was sent via e-mail through Constant Contact to a targeted database that contains Italian American organizations and individuals. A second reminder to fill out the questionnaire was sent a week after the initial questionnaire was sent. The questionnaire takes approximately fifteen to thirty minutes to complete. The questionnaire was compiled and sent out on March 21, 2016. This allowed for enough time to formulate interview questions based on answers obtained from the question-naire and to conduct face-to-face (or telephone) interviews. The interview stage part was completed by April 30, 2016.

The targeted audience for this proposed research was identified via the John D. Calandra Italian American Institute e-mail database of 8,594 contacts of Italian American organizations and Italian American individuals. In addition, the researcher's Facebook page of one 145 people was also used to publicize and encourage people to participate in the survey. The data collected from this research, such as ages of both male and female respondents, were examined together with how many first-, second-, and third-generation respondents take part. Tables were used to demonstrate the possible need for such a facility in New York City.

The methods used to conduct this research constitute a mixed methodology of both qualitative and quantitative methods. Demographic data were gathered. Simple descriptive statistics along with correlation were used to extract data.

RESEARCH CRITERIA

The research criteria for this project are individuals who are sixty-five years of age or older and of Italian descent living in New York City. Participants can be half Italian, or self-identify as Italian American. Subjects were identified through the Calandra Institute mailing list.

INSTRUMENTS

The instruments used to conduct this research include a questionnaire (see Appendix A) with open-ended questions such as the individual's view of nursing homes or any type of assisted living facilities. Follow-up interviews were conducted with some of the individuals who indicated they wanted to participate. Interview questions included: "What are your plans for the future?" "Do you think that there are Italian or Italian American values that influence how families manage elder care?" (see Appendix B) The research tools included public records such as Census data (American Community Survey covering one year 2014), Constant Contact for the questionnaire that was sent through the Calandra Institute's e-mail list, and the Facebook page of this researcher, which was used to post the questionnaire with a link to the Constant Contact sent out on the Calandra Institute e-mail database. The questionnaire was developed by the researcher based on the very limited published literature on this topic and the rest of the literature reviewed on ethnic elders. Follow-up interviews were conducted by the researcher. The interview questions were developed by the researcher based on the respondents' answers to the questionnaire.

DATA COLLECTION

Data collection began once completed questionnaires in Constant Contact were answered. Constant Contact is able to gather all data and formulate percentages of answers. Interview questions were sent out to those individuals who agreed to participate. The respondents were given several choices as to which method they preferred to be contacted for an interview the majority indicated email. The initial contact was made via e-mail, asking the participants if they were still interested in taking part in an interview regarding Italian American elder care. When respondents answered back they asked that the interview questions be sent directly to them. Once the interview questions were returned the researcher reviewed the respondents' answers and conducted in-person and telephone interviews.

DATA ANALYSIS

The researcher examined data collected from a questionnaire that calculates the percentage of answers performing descriptive statistics. This method allows for assessing the need of an Italian American nursing home or assisted living facility for Italian Americans who are sixty-five years and older who live in New York City. Tables demonstrate the data collected. Variables such as ethnicity and whether or not the subject is of Italian American descent are considered. Given the fact that this initial outreach is a pilot study, the follow-up process was analyzed to further assess the need for this facility. The researcher assumes that the respondents are the subjects that were intended for this research project (i.e., ethnicity, age) and that the respondents have some knowledge of computer use.

CHAPTER 4

FINDINGS

The questionnaire was sent out to a database of 8,594 people (Italian American organizations and Italian American individuals in the tri-state area); from the 8,594 recipients, 251 respondents attempted to answer the questionnaire — the criteria for answering questionnaire was age sixty-five years or older and a New York City resident. Out of the 251 respondents, 226 were eligible to answer the questionnaire, and from that number forty-five respondents completed the questionnaire.

TABLE 1. DEMOGRAPHIC DATA

Female	78.0%
Male	22.0%
First generation	38.6%
Second generation	38.0%
Third generation	22.7%
Fourth generation	2.0%
African American	0.0%
Asian	0.0%
Hispanic/Latino	2.0%
Italian	22.0%
Italian American	66.6%
White	8.8%
Other	8.8%
Married	48.8%
Divorced	8.8%
Widowed	20.0%
Single	26.6%
Children Yes	51.0%
Children No	49.0%

The demographic breakdown of the respondents showed that participants were 78 percent female and 22 percent male. The highest proportion of respondents was of the first generation (38.6 percent). Married respondents represented the largest proportion of participants (49 percent), followed by widowed participants (20 percent), divorced people (9 percent), and finally single people (27 percent). Fifty-one percent said they had children and 49 percent had no children.

TABLE 2. CURRENT LIVING SITUATION, WITH WHOM, HOW AND WHERE

Live alone Yes	43.0%
Live alone No	57.0%
Spouse	84.0%
Children	8.0%
Relative	4.0%
Sibling	4.0%
Friend	
Home	37.7%
Nursing home	0.0%
Assisted living facility	2.2%
Apartment building	37.7%
Condo	20.0%
Townhouse	4.4%

Respondents were asked to evaluate their living situation; 57 percent lived with someone. The majority of those living with someone lived with a spouse (84 percent). As for where they lived, data showed both in a house and/or apartment building were the same.

TABLE 3. WHAT KIND OF ARRANGEMENTS, IF ANY, ARE CURRENTLY IN PLACE FOR YOURSELF SHOULD YOU BECOME INCAPACITATED?

Go to a nursing home	6.5%
Stay at home with help from spouse and/or family	15.5%
Stay at home and have paid help	28.0%
Go live with a relative	0.0%
Go live with my children	2.0%
I currently have no arrangements in place	48.0%

Should they become incapacitated, 48 percent of respondents had no arrangements in place; 28 percent said they would stay at home and have paid help; 7 percent would go to a nursing home, and 2 percent would go live with their children.

TABLE 4. WHAT IS YOUR VIEW OF NURSING HOMES?

Good place to be if you have no one who can take care of you	40.0%
Horrible place; I would never want to end up there	50.0%
I have no view on nursing homes	6.6%
I don't know much about nursing homes	2.5%

TABLE 5. WHAT IS YOUR VIEW OF ASSISTED LIVING FACILITIES?

Good place to be if you have no one who can take care of you	66.5%
Horrible place; I would never want to end up there	2.2%
I have no view of assisted living facilities	6.5%
I don't know much about assisted living facilities	25.0%

We see that 66.5 percent of respondents said they saw assisted living facilities as a good place to be as opposed to the 40 percent who selected nursing homes. Fifty percent felt that nursing homes are a terrible place to be. The comments received on this were numerous:

- "Good nursing homes are expensive in order to provide adequately trained staff."

- "Nursing homes that are for the benefit of the owners, provide unskilled staff in insufficient numbers to provide necessary care for those living there."
- "I may end up in one, but hope not."
- "Hope to avoid it, if at all possible."

Comments on the subject of assisted living facilities:

- "Can be very lonely despite activities available."
- "Need to be researched thoroughly before making a decision."
- "I much prefer this to a nursing home. One that has different levels of living, from independent to assisted to nursing care."
- "If you can pay for a good one."

TABLE 6. WOULD YOU CONSIDER LIVING IN A NURSING HOME?

Yes	31.0%
No	69.0%

TABLE 7. IF NO, WHY NOT?

I want to be in my own home	68.0%
My family would abandon me and not visit me at all	0.0%
Other (please explain)	26.0%

Only 31 percent of participants said they would live in a nursing home. When answering as to why not, 68 percent said they wanted to be in their own home. Some comments received on this were:

- "It's like waiting for the grim reaper."

- "Both my wife and I, if possible, would rather have care at home. Brave words, but I have no idea how it all will work out."
- "I will postpone becoming 'inventory' for as long as I possibly can."

TABLE 8. WOULD YOU CONSIDER LIVING IN AN ASSISTED LIVING FACILITY?

Yes	77.0%
No	23.0%

TABLE 9. IF NO, WHY NOT?

I want to be in my own home	70.0%
My family would abandon me	0.0%
Other (please explain)	10.0%

Noted is that 77 percent said they would prefer assisted living over entering a nursing home.

TABLE 10. WOULD YOU CONSIDER LIVING IN A NURSING HOME OR ASSISTED LIVING FACILITY IF IT CATERED TO YOUR SPECIFIC ETHNIC BACKGROUND?

Yes	58.0%
No	36.0%

TABLE 11. WOULD YOU CONSIDER LIVING IN A NURSING HOME OR ASSISTED LIVING FACILITY IF THEIR CULTURAL ACTIVITIES ALSO REFLECTED YOUR OWN CULTURE?

Yes	60.4%
No	27.9%

When asked about considering a nursing home or assisted living facility that caters to one's ethnic and cultural background, 58 percent said they would be willing to enter an ethnic facility. Some comments on this were:

- "As I said, I would not consider living in a nursing home; however, if it was absolutely necessary I would certainly prefer living in one that catered to my ethnic background."

- "As far as I know, there aren't any Italian homes."

- "I would not want to live in a nursing home; however, I would consider living in an assisted living facility. In either case, something catering to my ethnic background would not be a prerequisite."

- "I so not want to be in a nursing home, however, if there were to be no other choice, it would be better if the majority of patients were to be Italian Americans."

- "Irrelevant to me."

- "Although this is not a requirement, it would be nice to be with people who shared a heritage with me. I find it increasingly difficult to meet Italian Americans who share the same memories growing up as 2nd generation Italo-Americans and I find almost no one who speaks Italian."

Of the respondents, 60.4 percent said that they would enter a facility that offers the same cultural activities as theirs. Some comments on this were:

- "To consider a nursing home is not about cultural activities. It is about being sick and no one available to take care of me or no one should since it would be a burden. And I suppose that if there were cultural activities that might ease the challenge of living in a nursing home."

- "This is not a primary concern for me and could be a negative if the cultural activities' focus was too (what I consider) heavy-handed."

- "Again, I would want to remain home with my family. I have only one daughter who feels the exact same way I do."

TABLE 12. HAVE YOU THOUGHT ABOUT THE COST OF LIVING IN A NURSING HOME OR ASSISTED LIVING FACILITY?

I can afford it if that is my choice	50.0%
It would be a financial hardship to pay for care in a facility	25.0%
It is too expensive for me to plan on seeking care in a facility	25.0%

TABLE 13. HOW MUCH DO YOU THINK IT COSTS PER YEAR TO LIVE IN A NURSING HOME OR ASSISTED LIVING FACILITY?

$50,000	16.0%
$75,000	20.0%
$100,000	15.0%
$125,000	4.5%
More than $125,000	40.0%

What is the cost involved in entering a nursing home or assisted living facility? Do they know the costs, and could they afford either one? Fifty percent said they would be able to afford either one; 25 percent said it would be a hardship and the other 25 percent said they would have to seek another type of care; 40 percent thought that the cost of entering either a nursing home or assisted living facility would be greater than $125,000 per year. Some of their comments:

- "If it is a permanent move, I would sell my house and use the proceeds to support myself in an appropriate facility. I would prefer to remain in my own home as long as possible."
- "This is something I would try to avoid at all costs."
- "I am 106 yrs old how much longer can I live that I could not afford it?"
- "At least now. With inflation, I'm not certain." "I know how much it costs — that's not the point!"

During the interviews conducted, respondents were asked to answer eleven questions. They were asked to describe such things as their living situations; what types of plans were in place for their future; their overall experience with elder care; whether or not their heritage played a role in how they view elder care; their thoughts on today's Italian American family values and why they thought that there is no nursing home in New York City that caters to the Italian American population. Given the brevity of time to conduct the interviews, only four were completed: This is not enough to make any clear assumptions. However, what was noted from these interviews was primarily the fact that all individuals talked about their families extensively; the interviews became a sort of therapy session for these four individuals. The respondents wanted to discuss this topic at length. It is also interesting that all four individuals interviewed talked about their grandparents and said that at one point or another the grandparents had lived with their family. All four respondents indicated that an ethnic facility would not be a deal-breaker for them; they showed a desire to be among their intellectual peers. As a matter of fact one respondent said: "They can keep the pastas and the little Italies. I want to be able to be around individuals who share my intellectual interests." Again, four interviews is not enough to produce any concrete assumptions but it does seem to support the findings of the questionnaire—that the elderly want to live independently and that having an ethnic medical facility is not relevant in making that type of decision.

LIMITATIONS

Some limitations for this study: Data were collected only from New York City residents who were sixty-five years and older. This drastically reduced the number of responses. The sample group was small, so perhaps not enough data were collected to make more reliable assumptions. Had the criteria of the questionnaire been left open for all Italian American individuals in the tri-state area regardless of age or residence status, more responses might have been received, which in turn would have yielded more data producing a different outcome. Additional limitations include the brevity of time researcher had to conduct interviews.

CHAPTER 5

DISCUSSION

The study found that the majority of Italian Americans still prefer to be in their own home as they move into old age and confront disease. Family bonds are still very strong. They prefer to live independently, and if they had to enter a nursing home they would consider entering one that catered to their ethnic and cultural background. In addition, the majority of respondents did not have any plans in case they become incapacitated.

The study also discovered not only the lack of literature on the subject of elder care amongst Italian Americans, but a lack of scholarly literature on elderly ethnic population overall in major developing countries. The literature reviewed pointed to several factors as to why this could be (Shah, Doe, & Deverill, 2008), one of which was lack of funds for research, language barriers, and the overall research structure such as organizations and institutions not being sensitive to ethnic elderly's difference and needs.

This study has generated much interest in the Italian American community in New York City. Members of the community who were not able to participate were frustrated that they could not respond to the questionnaire if they were not eligible, but still had a desire to express their feelings on this topic by emailing and phoning. They all thought this was an important topic and were glad that someone was "finally looking at it." This leads me to believe that the community is aware of the lack of information on this topic. The scholarly community on the other hand might not be. And so I have asked myself, why? Is it because

Italian Americans are looking at elder care differently than other ethnic groups? Asian Americans have been shown to have similar beliefs in regards to one's elders. They, however, have been active in this subject, whether it's the nursing home created by the Japanese community in Seattle as discussed in the literature review or the abundance of literature in scholarly journals and most notably on the AARP website, where one can find a whole section dedicated to the Asian American Community. There are reports on Filipino and Asian or Pacific Islanders elder care, caregivers, housing information, and the list goes on.

More research is recommended to cover the lack of scholarly literature on elderly ethnic minorities. Excluding a group that is increasing in numbers from the scholarly literature can only lead to misdiagnosis, lower quality of life, and less cost effective methods.

This study has just begun to scratch the surface on Italian American elder care. It is the first study that surveyed respondents who were sixty-five years and over. Past studies focused on the families and caretakers of Italian American elders, not the populace themselves. This was a direct way to discover from the elderly what their thoughts were on elder care and family traditions. According to the findings it seems that what the elders are saying is that they want to live independently and to not be dependent on their families, although the family bonds are still very strong. If an ethnic nursing home or assisted living facility exists it's irrelevant to them. The ways Italian American elders look at their care are no longer so traditional. More research is certainly recommended on the subject. It is recommended that the Italian American community mount a campaign to fund research to be conducted on this issue and to eventually establish an Italian American nursing home.

REFERENCES

American Association of Retired Persons. http://www.aarp.org/home-family/ friends-family/info-04-2013/three-generations-household-american-family. html?intcmp=AE-ASIANCOMM-LIFE. Retrieved April 20, 2016.

American Association of Retired Persons. http://www.aarp.org/research/ topics/ care/info-2016/aapi-chinese-filipino-caregiving-research.html?intcmp=AE-ASIANCOMM-NEWS. Retrieved April 20, 2016.

Cohen M. Z., Sansoni, J., & Vellone, E., (2002). The experience of Italians caring for family members with alzheimer's disease. *Journal of Nursing Scholarship*, 34, 323–329.

Colon, M. (2003). Comparison of hospice use and demographics among European Americans, African Americans, and Latinos. *American Journal of Hospice and Palliative Medicine*, 20(3), 182–190.

Degenholtz, H. B., Arnold, R. A., Meisel, A., & Lave, J. R. (2002). Persistence of racial disparities in advance care plan documents among nursing home residents. *Journal of the American Geriatrics Society*, 50(2), 378–381.

Duffy, S. A., Jackson, F. C., Schim, S. M., Ronis, D. L., & Fowler, K. E. (2006). Racial/ethnic preferences, sex preferences, and perceived discrimination related to end-of-life care. *Journal of the American Geriatrics Society*, 54(1), 150–157.

Fandetti, D. V., & Gelfand, D. E. (1976). Care of the aged attitudes of white ethnic families. *The Gerontologist*, 16(6), 544–549.

Gelfand, D. E., & Fandetti, D. V. (1980). Suburban and urban white ethnics: Attitudes towards care of the aged. *The Gerontologist*, 20(5 Part 1), 588–594.

Kolb, P.J., Hofstein, R., (2007) Italian American elders. In P.J. Kolb & R. Hofstein, (Eds.), *Social work practice with ethnically and racially diverse nursing home residents and their families* (pp. 107–131). New York, NY: Columbia University Press.

McCormick, W. C., Uomoto, J., Young, H., Graves, A. B., Vitaliano, P., Mortimer, J. A., & Larson, E. B. (1996). Attitudes toward use of nursing homes and home care in older Japanese-Americans. *Journal of the American Geriatrics Society*, 44(7), 769–777.

Mold, F. (2005). Minority ethnic elders in care homes: A review of the literature. *Age and Ageing*, 34(2), 107–113.

New York State Department of Health. https://www.health.ny.gov/facilities/ nursing/estimated_average_rates.htm. Retrieved April 15, 2016.

Shah, A., Doe, P., & Deverill, K. (2008). Ethnic minority elders: Are they neglected in published geriatric psychiatry literature? *International Psychogeriatrics*, 20(05).

Sons of Italy Senior Citizens Housing. http://section-8-housing.findthebest.com/ l/18433/Sons-of-Italy-Senior-Citizens-Housing. Retrieved April 11, 2016.

The United States Census Bureau. American Fact Finder (2014). http://factfinder2. census.gov/faces/tableservices/jsf/pages/ productview.xhtml?pid=ACS_11 _1YR_S2701andprodType. Retrieved April 15, 2016.

APPENDIX A

March 17th, 2016

Dear Friend,

My name is Rosaria and I am a graduate student working on a final project to complete my degree. When I was asked to think about my final project I knew instantly the subject of research I wanted to pursue—the types of elder care that are currently in place for Italian Americans. My own family experience with elder care was when my grandmother developed Alzheimer's. We chose to take care of her at home and not have her stay in a facility.

I have always wondered about the kinds of factors that influence such an important decision amongst Italian Americans. Is it a generational issue? What are the costs involved for any type of care? Is cost a factor that determines the type of care one will choose?

I would like to ask you to assist me in my research by taking a few moments to answer the enclosed questionnaire. The purpose of this questionnaire is to assess the current and potential needs of elder care among New York City's Italian Americans that are aged 65 and older. Your answers are strictly confidential.

Thank you in advance for your help.

Sincerely,
Rosaria Musco

ELDER CARE AMONGST ITALIAN AMERICANS QUESTIONNAIRE

Are you of age 65 or older?

□ Yes

□ No

If you are not of age 65 or older please do not go on.

Thank you for your time.

Do you currently reside in New York City?

□ Yes

□ No

If your answer is no, please do not go on.

Thank you for your time.

What is your date of birth? _____

What is your generation of Italian heritage?

□ First Generation

□ Second Generation

□ Third Generation

□ Fourth Generation

Your gender:

□ Male

□ Female

Where were you born? _____

What is your ethnic background?

☐ African American

☐ Asian

☐ Hispanic/Latino

☐ Italian

☐ Italian American

☐ White

☐ Other

What language do you prefer to speak?

☐ English

☐ Italian

☐ French

☐ Spanish

☐ Other

Aside from your preferred language, how many other languages do you speak if any, and what are they?

☐ English

☐ Italian

☐ French

☐ Spanish

☐ Other (please list) _____

☐ No other language aside from English

Marital Status

☐ Married

☐ Divorced

☐ Widowed

☐ Single

Do you have children?

□ Yes

□ No

Do you live alone? Yes □ No □

If you do not live alone, with whom do you live or who lives with you?

□ Spouse

□ Children

□ Sibling

□ Relative

What type of dwelling do you live in?

□ Home

□ Nursing home

□ Assisted living facility

□ Apartment building

□ Condo

□ Townhouse

What kind of arrangements if any are currently in place for yourself should you become incapacitated?

□ Go to a nursing home

□ Stay at home with help from spouse and or family

□ Stay at home and have paid help

□ Go live with my children

□ Go live with a relative

What is your view of nursing homes? Please check all that apply.

☐ Good place to be if you have no one who can take care of you

☐ Horrible place; I would never want to end up there.

☐ I have no view on nursing homes.

☐ I don't know much about nursing homes.

☐ Other.

What is your view of assisted living facilities?

☐ Good place to be if you have no one who can take care of you.

☐ Horrible place; I would never want to end up there.

☐ I have no view of assisted living facilities.

☐ I don't know much about assisted living facilities.

☐ Other.

Have you ever visited a nursing home or assisted living facility?

☐ No

☐ Yes (explain which facility and what you thought of it):

_____

Do you currently know anyone (family, friends) who lives in a nursing home or assisted living facility in the New York area?

☐ Yes ☐ No

Would you consider living in a nursing home?

☐ Yes

☐ No

If not, why not?

□ I want to be in my own home.

□ My family would abandon me and not visit me at all.

□ Other (please explain):

_____

Would you consider living in an assisted living facility?

□ Yes

□ No

If not, why not?

□ I want to be in my own home.

□ My family would abandon me and not visit me at all.

□ Other (please explain):

_____

Would you consider living in a nursing home or assisted living facility if it catered to your specific ethnic background?

□ Yes

□ No

Would you consider living in a nursing home or assisted living facility if the staff's facility, aside from speaking English, also spoke your preferred language?

□ Yes

□ No

Would you consider living in a nursing home or assisted living facility if their cultural activities also reflected your own culture?

□ Yes

□ No

How do you think about the cost of living in a nursing home or assisted living facility?

□ I can afford it if that is my choice.

□ It would be a financial hardship to pay for care in a facility.

□ It is too expensive for me to plan on seeking care in a facility.

How much do you think it costs per year to live in a nursing home or assisted living facility?

□ $50,000

□ $75,000

□ $100,000

□ $125,000

Did anyone other than yourself help you fill out this questionnaire?

□ Yes

□ No

If yes, who was it?

□ Spouse

□ Children

□ Sibling

□ Friend

What is the best way to contact you for a brief follow up interview?

☐ Telephone # _____

☐ E-Mail address _____

☐ I do not wish to be contacted

APPENDIX B

ITALIAN AMERICANS ELDER CARE INTERVIEW QUESTIONS

1) Describe your living situation.

2) What are your plans for the future? Tell me why you have made these plans. If no plans, tell my why you have not made any plans.

3) What would affect the plans that you have made or that you think you would make?

4) What has been your family, friends, neighbors' experience with elder care?

5) Is that experience something that you envision for yourself?

6) Do you think that financially you will be able to cover your medical costs and other needs as time goes on?

7) Do you think your cultural heritage has had a role to play in how you think about elder care? If so, how?

8) Do you think there are Italian or Italian American values that influence how families manage elder care?

9) Based on the answers of the questionnaire sent out, the majority of Italian American elders viewed entering into a nursing home a death sentence. Do you feel the same way?

10) Do you think that besides providing adequate care if a nursing home provided ethnic and cultural activities that reflected your own it would make entering a nursing or assisted living facility easier?

11) What are your thoughts on today's Italian American family values?

12) Why do you think that currently no Italian American nursing homes exist in New York City?

INDEX